Coordinated Management of Meaning (CMM)
A Research Manual

Natasha A. Rascon &
Stephen W. Littlejohn

Taos Institute Publications
Chagrin Falls, Ohio
USA

Coordinated Management of Meaning (CMM)
A Research Manual

Cover and Design Layout: Deborah Stocco

Taos Institute Publications
A Division of the Taos Institute
Chagrin Falls, Ohio
USA

ISBN-13: 978-1-938552-60-1
LCCN: 2017952690

Printed in the USA and in the UK

Introduction to
Taos Institute Publications

The Taos Institute is a nonprofit organization dedicated to the development of social constructionist theory and practice for purposes of world benefit. Constructionist theory and practice locate the source of meaning, value, and action in communicative relations among people. Our major investment is in fostering relational processes that can enhance the welfare of people and the world in which they live. Taos Institute Publications offers contributions to cutting-edge theory and practice in social construction. Our books are designed for scholars, practitioners, students, and the openly curious public. The **Focus Book Series** provides brief introductions and overviews that illuminate theories, concepts, and useful practices. The **Tempo Book Series** is especially dedicated to the general public and to practitioners. The **Books for Professionals Series** provides in-depth works that focus on recent developments in theory and practice. **WorldShare Books** is an online offering of books in PDF format for free download from our website. Our books are particularly relevant to social scientists and to practitioners concerned with individual, family, organizational, community, and societal change.

— Kenneth J. Gergen
President, Board of Directors
The Taos Institute

For information about the Taos Institute and social constructionism visit:
www.taosinstitute.net

Table of Contents

PREFACE: CMM as Research

IN 2008, BARNETT PEARCE WROTE a chapter, "Doing Research in our Right Minds." In that chapter, he posed the question: Can research help us develop new ways of relating to each other and to the world around us that are commensurate with the new capacities it has conferred? Or must we look elsewhere for the wisdom we need to use our knowledge? This question is performative in contrast to informing which is, an enactment of the communication perspective, and the Coordinated Management of Meaning, CMM. It makes the distinction "between research that helps us do the same things better and research that helps us do better things, i.e., ...so rather than fight wars in new places such as outer space, we engage in a process of learning how to make peace so that we don't need new weapons when we move into outer space (Pearce, 2007, pp. 6-12).

This volume for the Focus Book Series on the uses and applications of the Coordinated Management of Meaning does just that. Rascon and Littlejohn have done a comprehensive work of introducing the reader to the history and development of using CMM and communication perspective in research, key concepts how this approach differs from other approaches, and offers tools and methods to support the reader who is ready to use CMM as a research method.

As practitioners joining the discourse of scholars, we both learned the value of CMM as theory and as method in our pursuits. We welcome this Focus Book as a resource to those who approach research from a social construction perspective and who will join and contribute to how we understand our social worlds. And for the reader who is interested in learning more about CMM, we invite you to read our book, published by Taos Institute Publications. It is a brief introduction to CMM. *Communicating Possibilities: A Brief Introduction to the Coordinated Management of Meaning (CMM)*. You can find it at: www.taosinstitute.net/focus-books-tempo-books-professional-books

~Ilene Wasserman and Beth Fisher-Yoshida; Co-Editors, CMM Focus Book Series

INTRODUCTION

"[I]F YOU ARE READING THESE words, you probably already know something about the Coordinated Management of Meaning – CMM – and are interested in exploring new and different ways to use it" (Sostrin, Pearce, & Pearce 2011, p. 4).

Like the Field Guide in which the above statement appears, this manual is primarily for scholars who wish to use CMM tools, but with a slightly different focus: instead of being used in a consulting context, this manual is designed for researchers. We hope to provide an adequate overview of CMM theory, research design considerations, and research tools.

The power of reflexivity, a central concept in CMM, can be seen throughout this work, and we encourage all CMM researchers to work in a self-reflexive manner, always questioning their own role in the research and ways in which the research process itself impacts them as researchers and communicators.

Although you will find research discussions in a wide variety of sources, we particularly recommend Barnett Pearce's papers,

"Using CMM" and "Doing Research from the Perspective of the Coordinated Management of Meaning (CMM)." These are available through the CMM Institute for Personal and Social Evolution and the CMM Archives at Fitchburg State University.

This booklet is the product of a doctoral course on CMM research tools that the two of us completed together with a dear friend, Nicholas Noblet. We looked at Pearce's articles on the subject and a variety of other sources and decided to share what we learned in a relatively simple, practical format. The CMM Institute, of which we are associates, provides the perfect outlet for this material.

This manual is not intended to be all-inclusive. CMM is complex, multi-dimensional, and constantly changing. Here we present some basics that should be a good starting place for CMM researchers. You should adapt, modify, and add to these tools as needed for your own work.

We would like to thank our colleagues from the CMM Institute and especially Beth Fisher-Yoshida for her help in editing this book. Lastly, we would like to extend a special gratitude to our colleague Nick for his contributions to this manual.

Natasha A. Rascon, Stephen Littlejohn
Albuquerque, New Mexico, 2017.

1 | CMM OVERVIEW

IF YOU ARE USING CMM as a research methodology, you probably already know quite a bit about the theory. You will find ample published resources about the theory itself if you wish to pursue it in greater detail. We list a few places to start at the end of this section; each of these publications will lead you to others. A good resource would be the companion to this book, a Taos Institute Publication by Ilene Wasserman and Beth Fisher-Yoshida, *Communicating Possibilities: A Brief Introduction to the Coordinated Management of Meaning (CMM)* (2017). Here we provide just a basic overview.

A Little History

The Theory of the Coordinated Management of Meaning emerged in the 1970s with several publications by W. Barnett Pearce, Vernon Cronen, and their students at the University of Massachusetts. The theory was first codified at length in Pearce & Cronen's *Communication, Action, and Meaning* in 1980 and expanded in many other publications since then.

Featuring the idea that communication is a process of making meaning in social interaction, the theory quickly became a standard in the communication theory canon. Although the major concepts in Pearce and Cronen's 1980 book remain central to the theory, these have expanded significantly to include a variety of new ideas related to the theme of coordinated meaning and action.

Initially, the theory was offered as a way of understanding communication as a systemic process of interaction and coordination. It quickly emerged as a practical theory designed to provide insights into how communicators might manage situations more effectively and thereby participate in the creation of better social worlds. To this end, a variety of studies of family systems, moral conflict, public discourse, and other topics appeared over the years.

Pearce's 1989 text *Communication and the Human Condition* enhanced and broadened the theory by elaborating the three central ideas now considered as the framework for CMM—coordination, coherence, and mystery.

The most recent book that explains this action orientation in depth is Pearce's 2007 volume *Making Social Worlds*. Today, the theory has many adherents throughout the world. The Institute for Personal and Social Evolution was founded in 2011 as a home for "all things CMM." The advent of the CMM Archives at Fitchburg State University provides an important repository and resource for CMM practitioners and scholars.

Philosophical Orientation

As a theory of systemic social constructionism, CMM is based on the interactional nature of reality, or the idea that our realities are constituted in communication. Our communication—words and ges-

2

tures—creates, shapes, and changes our shared realities. A thing is no longer objectively described from a bystander's point of view, but is constructed in its expressions. Although individual speech acts are part of this construction process, meaning is never complete outside of interaction, the give and take of verbal and nonverbal acts. For these reasons, CMM is strongly based in system theory and relational communication theory.

Communication can be thought of as a reflexive cycle involving practices and resources, in which actions create meanings and meanings in turn shape actions. One takes a communication perspective by looking at this reflexive, interactional process. Any human activity can be viewed from the communication perspective in this way. According to Pearce (1989), "[i]n this sense, 'practices' consist in actions such as building a bridge, playing bridge, and seeking to bridge misunderstandings; 'resources' comprise the stories, images, symbols, and institutions that persons use to make their world meaningful" (p. 23).

CMM is a practical theory. Cronen and others have distinguished practical theory from foundationalist theories by noting the implications of practical theory for action. Instead of making general predictive statements about communication, CMM provides a set of concepts and relations that can be used to make decisions about how one might navigate complex life situations. For this reason, most CMM research is situation-centered and case-based.

The theory does not provide causal laws that predict outcomes, but assumes that actors must make decisions in a multi-valued world, in which numerous outcomes are possible, some more desirable than others. Hence, CMM finds roots in American pragmatism, particularly in symbolic interaction and the social construction of reality.

3

CMM does make some universal statements, but these are always conclusions that do not govern, but describe. CMM contends, for example, that across situations people use various logics to understand their own and others' actions, that they act based on these logics, that meanings are always understood within a constantly changing landscape of contexts, and that communication always consists of some attempt to coordinate, which may be constructive or not. These kinds of statements are not intended to describe the entire universe of possible conceptions, but to offer one set of concepts believed to be highly useful in understanding and acting in communication. The theory acknowledges that all theories have limits, that no system of ideas can be complete, and that mystery is always present in the affairs of human beings. Thus, meanings are always open, making CMM a generative theory.

Some Key Concepts

This manual is not intended to be a short course in CMM. Some familiarity is presumed, but we do feel that a brief overview of some core concepts would be helpful. Each of the following concepts is more complex than implied here, and you can read more about these in other sources.

Coordination, Coherence, Mystery

Taken together, these three concepts provide a basic framework for CMM.

In sum, **coordination** is the process of meshing or organizing actions within an episode or interaction. **Coherence** is understanding or meaning in the interaction, often expressed in stories; and **mystery**

4

is the knowledge of limitations, that no matter how many stories we accrue, there are more to be understood and available in our larger world. These three terms make up the **communication perspective**.

These three "big ideas" of CMM provide a high-level touchstone for evaluating communication patterns and episodes. For example, researchers might ask whether certain episodes are coordinated or not. How might the lack of coordination frustrate or confuse communicators? If an episode is highly coordinated, do participants find this a happy state or a frustrating one? Is the episode coherent to the participants, and do they share coherence or meaning? Is there sufficient mystery in the interaction or situation to open avenues for change, stimulate imagination, and enhance communicators' stories of what is happening?

Meaning and Action

The tight connection between meaning and action is a mainstay of CMM. The idea here is that meaning affects action and, reflexively, action shapes meaning. How we understand a situation shapes our responses within that situation, and our responses shape how we view it. Consistently, CMM prefers loops and circles to lines. Pearce has referred to the meaning action loop as a connection between resources (our meanings) and practices (our actions).

Borrowing from speech act theory, CMM explains meaning and action in terms of constitutive and regulative rules. A constitutive rule, or **meaning rule**, tells you what an act (including a speech act) counts as, what it means. A regulative, or **action rule**, identifies how one should act or respond to another act. These two types of rules guide an individual in understanding and behaving within an episode or interaction. Meaning and action rules are highly contextual, and they can shift and change from moment to moment and from situation to situation. For example, most of the time "How are you?" counts as a greeting, and one is obligated to respond by saying, "Fine." However, if the communicators are close friends and one has a serious illness, "How are you?" counts as a genuine inquiry into the others health, and the response will be quite different.

In general, we can think of meanings as resources that guide action and action as practices that influence resources. The resource-practice loop is a more elaborate depiction of the meaning-action loop described above (Pearce, 1989, p. 24).

The connection between meaning and action also has a hierarchy in which meanings and actions always entail one another. Each context is understood as part of another context. For example, the "self" may be understood as part of the "relationship," which in turn could be part of "culture."

However, contexts are dynamic; they can and do change. Indeed, communicators can choose to shift their own contexts of meaning and action and can do so to change communication patterns that are not working. Contexts are reflexive, meaning that contexts affect one another. You cannot continually go upward in a context hierarchy. At some point, you begin to come back down again. For example, you may understand the self within the context of a particular relationship, but at other times, come to view the relationship within the context of self.

Contexts are important in part because they provide logical force that connects meaning and action. A **logical force** is a sense that, given certain meanings within a set of contexts, there is pressure, or set of rules, to respond or act in certain ways. Thus, one's meaning and action rules arise out of certain logical forces that are in play.

6

Interaction

Although CMM research may begin with questions about individual meaning and action, it never stops there, but expands to larger units of interaction between or among individuals. On a higher level, such analysis can also look at interaction between social units such as groups, organizations, communities, or institutions.

CMM usually analyzes interaction by looking at larger and larger segments of talk, including acts, interacts, triplets, episodes, and forms. When thinking about communication, an act can be understood as one contributing factor to a conversation. One might choose to look at how one element of the entire conversation was more important than other acts in the conversation. For instance, when looking at college students that donate blood, the act in the overall context could be one student giving blood during a blood drive for the first time. An interact focuses on two elements that occur in sequence in the conversation. After identifying one act, another plays into the original act, creating an interact. In the same context, when the student arrives to donate blood, the volunteer explains the process in a clear and informative manner. Extending on two acts, a triplet involves the two elements of the interact and an additional act in the same sequence of the conversation. In the example after understanding the process, the student then consents to donating blood. There are other acts in the example that can be considered as well.

Many acts occur when looking at the process of donating blood; you might first consider the student arriving at the location and end the consideration when the student leaves the location. The compilation of the many acts in the context of donating blood is an example of an episode of communication.

Also important to consider is the future episodes of interaction that the student will experience. In future years when the student has donated blood several times, each time is an episode of interaction of the larger conversational context of donating blood. An episode can be understood as a part of a larger conversational context. Each episode will be different from a previous or future episode for several reasons. One important reason is the way the individuals involved choose to engage in the conversation. Several factors can be considered, including, for example, communicating in a (dis)respectful way, being open- or closed-minded, and acknowledging difference or failing to do so. Utilizing these factors demonstrates the form of communication that people exhibit, which can determine the (un) successful outcome of the interaction.

Forms of Communication

Four broad forms of communication are monocultural, ethnocentric, modernistic, and cosmopolitan. Each of these possesses special characteristics and reflects different views of self and other. In each of these forms, resources are protected or put at risk in various ways. In CMM, resources are meanings, rules, and forces on which people come to rely. Thus, when resources are at risk, our ways of understanding and acting can be threatened by others who have different ways of understanding and acting.

In **monocultural communication**, we are living in one world in which everyone is like us, and there is no threat to our resources (meanings, ways of understanding and acting). In this state, people do not acknowledge the presence of outside groups or different forms of communication. Everyone is treated as a native, and no resources are at risk.

In **ethnocentric communication**, we are aware and potentially threatened by people not like us who challenge our ways of understanding and acting. Ethnocentric communication acknowledges the presence of outside ways, but protects resources by building a wall between the groups. There is a clear distinction between natives and non-natives in this form.

In **modernistic communication**, sometimes referred to as "intercultural," we are very much aware of difference and realize its value. We seek it out in order to expand our own resources and practices. Modernity acknowledges the differences inherent in society but does not attach value, thereby lending itself to escalating relativism. Resources are constantly at risk due to the positive value placed on change. In modernistic communication, ways of understanding and acting are situated in a context in which change is valued, always necessitating new ones.

Finally, **cosmopolitan communication** acknowledges differences, seeks to understand the difference and engage in a different pattern with unfamiliar or changed resources, and then return to familiar territory with a more informed set of resources.

Dialogue

In general, CMM uses the term "better social world" to imply conditions in which human beings are respected and acknowledged, a world in which participants honor multiple perspectives and values, and a kind of communication in which people value their own resources and practices while working to understand and sometimes even adopt resources and practices of others. What forms of communication provide the great opportunity to make such better social worlds? Cosmopolitan communication is idealized in this regard. Pearce and others began in the 1990s to describe this kind of communication as dialogue. Martin Buber referred to this state as walking the narrow ridge between self and other. CMM says that it involves holding your own ground while remaining profoundly open to the other.

Stories

Stories, or narratives, have a long tradition in communication and related fields. Stories are a central investigative tool to uncover meanings and the processes that (re)create them. The definition of narrative, as found in Fisher (1984), is "...a theory of symbolic actions-words and/or deeds-that have sequence and meaning for those who live, create, or interpret them" (p. 2). Pearce (1989) states that "[t] he quality of the stories we tell determines whether we confront the facts of life with equanimity, ecstasy, or dread" (p. 69). CMM places a unique value on stories as statements of meaning, and their value in CMM methodology is crucial towards building better, and more coordinated, social worlds.

In recent work, Pearce's *Making Social Worlds* (2007) places particular value on stories as a vehicle of meaning expression. Beyond the assumption that all people are shaped by stories of culture, Pearce highlights the tension between lived and told stories in the LUUUUTT model. LUUUTT stands for stories Lived, Unknown stories, Untold stories, Unheard stories, Untellable stories, stories Told, and story-Telling. This model allows for exploration of complex stories, to fill in the gaps with hidden stories, and further develop the vocalized stories in the current way the story is being told to enhance and further the understanding of the meaning being made (Wasserman & Fisher-Yoshida, 2017). Another assumption of all people is that we are trying to tell ourselves stories that function in coherence and those stories are consistent enough with lived episodes to make them understand-

10

able. The communication perspective, then, sees stories as something universal among people, powerful to convey meaning, and able to express understandings that might otherwise remain hidden.

Why are stories important to you as a researcher? They are useful in CMM as a tool to get at meaning; that is, you can use stories (in solicitation of or concert with others) to expose concepts of CMM within everyday narratives. For example, you might inquire about the story of how a person came to love or hate working at a job; this story not only contains coordination, coherence and mystery, but it also demonstrates the social world under constant construction in which the person lives. The concepts of CMM can be identified through stories, allowing researchers to get the process of making meaning and potentially open avenues for understanding and/or improving it. Remember, "...we live in communication" (Pearce, 1989, p. xvi).

SEAVA

SEAVA is a useful process originally designed for consulting, in which a practitioner leads a group through a series of reflections to raise awareness of what is happening from a communication perspective and to make plans for improved communication in the future. However, the SEAVA process is equally useful in research to learn more about group experiences from a communication perspective. The SEAVA process is best described in a two-part manual written by Sostrin, Pearce, and Pearce, entitled *CMM Solutions* (2011).

SEAVA is a set of stages in which various CMM tools are used. SEAVA stands for (1) storyboarding, (2) enriching, (3) analyzing, (4) visioning, and (5) acting. Although this sequence is logical, it does not need to be followed strictly as a prescribed sequence; it can be iterative, or flow in a non-sequential manner. Indeed, in this manual, we show how various tools can be used together or in isolation. Because this process employs many tools across the spectrum of description, interpretation, critique, and action, we explore the research potential later in this volume.

NOREN

NOREN is a new resource that describes a process of reflective think-ing in unique contexts (Wasserman & Fisher-Yoshida, 2017). NOREN stands for (1) Noticing, (2) Observing, (3) Reflecting, (4) Engaging, and (5) Noticing (Again). Noticing is the process of becoming aware or developing awareness. This first step begins the process of shifting to the third-person perspective to look at patterns of communication. Resonance and dissonance occur in this beginning phase and allow for a shift in perspective to commence. Helpful CMM tools during this phase are episodes, logical force, and mystery. The second step of the process expands on the third-person perspective of stepping back. Researchers observe and engage in those moments that they are a part of constructing. The observations are enhanced by con-sidering the complexity of the meaning being made and considering hierarchies of meaning, missing stories (LUUUUTT), logical force, and the order of events (serpentine model) in the episodes of interac-tion. Next, reflecting allows for choices to be identified. Researchers understand the patterns created either support or reinforce their belief systems. A main element of this phase is utilizing CMM models simultaneously to overcome an ethnocentric perspective of "us" versus "them". This step is followed by creating mindfulness in the engaging step. By looking at large and small systems ant what hap-pens in between and within the systems, researcher create coherence. When the goal of coherence is achieved, other questions emerge and the process of noticing occurs again. CMM researchers in this stage understand that episodes shift simply because they were noticed and a change in perspective often requires gaining another perspective to expand understanding.

The NOREN process is best described in the companion book, *Communicating Possibilities*, by Wasserman and Fisher-Yoshida (2017). Wasserman and Fisher-Yoshida's book is a qualitative inquiry enacting the NOREN process. Their example weaved throughout the text provides a clear demonstration of the process in a unique situation; social worlds are explored, a communication perspective is taken, critical moments and choices are revealed, and a variety of tools and frameworks are incorporated that demonstrate a clear CMM worldview.

Additional Resources on CMM

Cronen, V. (2001). Practical theory, practical art, and the pragmatic-systemic account of inquiry, *Communication Theory*, 11, 14-35.

Cronen, V.E. & Pearce, W.B. (1981). Logical force in interpersonal communication: A new concept of the 'necessity' in social behavior," *Communication*, 6, 5-67.

Littlejohn, S. W. (2009). Coordinated management of meaning. In S. W. Littlejohn & K. A. Foss, (Ed.), *Encyclopedia of Communication Theory* (vol. 1, pp. 200-203). Thousand Oaks, CA: Sage.

Pearce, W. B. (1989). *Communication and the human condition.* Carbondale, IL: Southern Illinois University Press.

Pearce, W. B. (2007). *Making social worlds: A communication perspective.* Malden, MA: Blackwell Publishing Limited.

Pearce, W.B., & Cronen, V.E. (1980). *Communication, action and meaning: The creation of social realities.* NY: Praeger.

Pearce, B., Sostrin, J., & Pearce, K. (2011). *CMM solutions: field guide for consultants.* USA: You Get What You Make Publishing.

Wasserman, I., & Fisher-Yoshida, B. (2017). *Communicating Possibilities: A Brief Introduction to the Coordinated Management of Meaning (CMM),* Chagrin Falls, OH: Taos Institute Publications

2 | POSITIONING THE RESEARCH

The Communication Perspective

At base, all CMM research takes a communication perspective. We can look at virtually anything from a communication perspective, but always this means that we (1) use a construction, rather than a transmission, model and (2) we look at the interaction itself rather than through it to something else.

Construction Model

The commonly used **transmission model** sees communication as tool for sending information and influencing people and groups. This useful model has been amply researched in other traditions. However, CMM takes a very different approach.

The **construction model,** used by CMM, is based on theories of social constructionism. In the model, communication is a process in which we create social worlds. This means that in one form or another, all CMM research asks two questions:

1. What is being made?

2. How is this being made in communication?

CMM research can go a step further to ask:

3. How can participants make something that works better for them?

Research that relies on the transmission model frequently addresses questions related to the effectiveness and accuracy of communication transmission. Questions related to clarity, accuracy, and channels of communication are common.

In contrast, research that relies on the construction model more typically looks at the nature of interaction and what this interaction accomplishes (or makes) within specific contexts. Such research would more likely address questions of the language of interaction, forms of speech employed, and participants. It frequently looks at speech acts, relationships, episodes, identities, and cultures.

Looking At Communication, Not Through It

When researchers use the construction model, they must look at the process of communication itself. This means that the data for CMM research is always interactional, always capturing a process occurring between and among participants.

Suppose, for example, that a researcher is interested in the effects of certain classroom communication methods on student learning. Using a transmission model, the researcher would look at two things—(1) the particular methods of communication and (2) measures of student outcomes. A CMM researcher would ask a different question: How are student and teacher understandings of learning shaped by the interaction patterns occurring in instructional settings?

The data would consist of actual interaction patterns and the meanings (or resources) and actions arising from these.

What CMM Research Is Not

CMM research is not:

- **Individual psychological analysis**—*Looks through communication at individual states and traits.*

- **Message analysis and message strategy analysis**—*Analyzes messages without examining interaction itself as the primary data, or treats the message separate from its context.*

- **Social Structural analysis**—*Focuses on institutions and larger social forms, but does not look at how these get made in social interaction.*

- **Effects and outcomes**—*Interested in how communication impacts individuals, groups, and audiences, but the focus is not on HOW these effects are actually made in episodes of interaction.*

- **Causal relations**—*Tries to establish universal or probabilistic cause-effect correlations among variables and does not acknowledge the rich differences in what gets made in different communication situations and, more importantly, how these relationships are made.*

This list is not meant to imply that CMM researchers would never be interested in psychology, messages, structure, effects, or causation, but they would conceptualize these quite differently as meanings and actions created in patterns of interaction, in which what gets made will vary over time and from one case to another.

Types and Stages: The DICA Model

CMM may be of four types:

1. Description

2. Interpretation

3. Critique

4. Action

We call this model DICA. These categories can also be thought of as stages of research. Although CMM could be used just to describe an interaction pattern, it normally goes beyond description to higher levels of analysis. A particular research study may stop at interpretation, but it may also go on to include critique and action, depending on the objectives of the researcher.

Description

The first step in the DICA model is to describe what is happening in an interaction or episode. Here data is used to identify patterns of interaction. Questions like these will help guide the descriptive stage:

1. What is happening here?

2. How are participants responding to one another?

3. How do participants understand what is happening?

4. What patterns are apparent over time?

You might use observations, recordings, transcripts, documents, or interviews to answer these questions.

Interpretation

In this stage, researchers use CMM tools to understand the social worlds being created, reinforced, or changed in the interaction under consideration.

Here are some guiding questions:

1. What do participants make of their situation?
2. What logics seem to be guiding their actions?
3. What contexts of meaning and action are prevalent here?
4. What social world is being made?

Critique

The third stage is critique. Here the researcher, often in collaboration with participants, identifies problems, challenges, and difficulties associated with the patterns of communication described. Here, you would look at questions like these:

1. How do participants describe and explain their problems?
2. What is not working well?
3. What is working well?
4. What do participants and others wish would happen?
5. What kind of social world do participants want?

Action

The last stage of research is action. This phase may or may not apply to your research design depending on the focus, but in this phase the researcher applies the generated social worlds and puts them into active practice. This could be considered an equivalent to action research, in which the researcher actively engages in reflexive execution of findings and results of data analysis. Some questions to consider at this phase are:

1. What communicative actions could create the social world(s) participants prefer?

2. What choices do they have? How can they make better choices?

3. How can the conversation change to better reflect outcomes of analyzed data?

RESEARCH EXAMPLE

Littlejohn, Shailor, and Pearce (1994) conducted eight case studies of mediation at the University of Massachusetts. The aim of the overall series was to determine the social worlds created in these mediations and to look at alternative ways in which disputants and mediators might better achieve coherent, coordinated outcomes.

In an attempt to **describe** the interaction patterns of the mediations, the researchers observed each session through a one-way mirror, while video-taping the mediation. They then viewed the videos and described the patterns they observed, using their fieldnotes and video observations. They took special note of the interaction among disputants and mediators as well as that between the mediators during private caucuses.

The researchers then made an **interpretive move** by describing the apparent underlying realities created and used by participants in the mediations, using a three-fold interpretive model. The three types of reality included a *moral reality*, or a sense of right and wrong; a *conflict reality*, or ideas about what constitutes a conflict; and a *justice reality*, or a sense of what is fair or not fair. In their studies, they found numerous examples of differing realities that either fueled the conflicts or made resolution more difficult.

In the **critical** part of the study, the researchers identified areas of confusion and a lack of coordination resulting from differing realities at the table. Each case had its own difficulties, of course, and some were more successful than others. However, a relatively common pattern involved mediators unconsciously siding with certain disputants because of a shared set of realities. Because these social realities lay at a deep level, mediators thought they could maintain neutrality, when in fact they were aligning rather significantly with one side or the other. In general, mediators treated the disputes primarily as substantive, issue-related conflicts without recognizing the deep realities that underscored the disagreements.

In an **action** stage, the researchers looked at various choices available to participants in working with disparate social realities and advocated the use of coordinated solutions that would not require a common understanding on the part of disputants. This would mean finding a relatively high-level frame that each party could relate to, each in his or her own way. The researchers suggested changes in mediator behavior that might make this kind of outcome possible.

Reflexivity in CMM Research

Traditionally, research has been viewed as an objective process in which the researcher maintains some "distance." Research is seen as a linear process of moving from question to answer. In contrast, CMM takes a wholly different approach to design.

CMM researchers usually practice continual reflexivity. Within CMM, reflexivity is important to gain deeper understanding of communication and its relationship to a variety of contexts. The understanding that the research question and answer process is not solely linear and one-way allows researchers to discuss findings and involve research participants in a new way, simply by focusing on reflexivity. Researchers might ask:

How does my interaction with other investigators affect my concept of process?

How does my interaction with participants affect my understanding of research, both as an idea and process?

How do the findings presented affect my position as an investigator?

What effect will my research have on all of the conversations I am currently engaged in?

From a systemic social construction perspective, the researcher knows from the outset that he or she is part of a larger system of relationships that constantly affect and are affected by one another. You cannot separate yourself from research questions, processes, or findings. Instead of seeing research as linear and objective, CMM scholars treat it as a set of ongoing conversations, and they use CMM itself as a way to understand the very research process in which they are engaged.

Thus, for example, research proceeds within a set of contexts in which the data "speaks." The researcher is in conversation with the data. In a reflexive hermeneutical fashion, researchers ask questions that elicit certain forms of data. The data provide answers, which brings the researcher back to new interpretations. As a CMM researcher, you would always leave the path of the research somewhat open, as new interpretations may lead to new research actions.

You can think of research as a set of decisions that shape and reflect the conversations of which they are part. Certainly, one of our important conversations is with CMM theory itself and the body of research that has been done. This would probably not be an important conversation if we were doing this research from a different perspective.

The CMM conversation privileges a certain set of principles, design considerations, and data types, and your research is then shaped in part by this hierarchy of meaning and action. At the top level of context, researcher(s) must consider the principles they are utilizing, for example:

Will this be a descriptive, interpretive, or critical study?

What traditions or perspectives will inform this design reflexively?

How will the research design inform data collection and analysis reflexively?

1. What will count as data in this research design?
2. What tools will I employ to gather my data?
3. What counts as data in my research?
4. What descriptions should I be seeking for my research?
5. Who or what am I interested in?
6. What are my research questions?

7. What conversation am I having with my data?

8. What social worlds are being made as a result of this data?

9. What interesting insights can my CMM tools provide me?

10. How do I need to format my data such that it is ready for analysis?

11. How can I enrich my data?

Then, they must create a design in line with those higher-level principles. In working the design, the researcher may find that the principles change. Finally, within the design, the researcher must decide what counts as data and what data count as. In other words, what are you looking at and what do you take that data to mean?

Community-Based Action Research

Community-Based Action Research occurs when the researcher joins with a group to achieve a positive outcome on behalf of the community. The researcher takes a facilitative role and may assume leadership in collecting data, but the project and outcomes are a joint endeavor. In the process of working together on a project, researchers and participants ask relevant questions, gather data, interpret that data, and make decisions about how to move forward. This kind of work is research embedded in an action project. The insights gained serve the community itself. Certainly not all CMM research is participatory in this sense, but CMM is well suited for this kind of work.

Taking a reflexive role in communication leads the researcher(s) in this kind of inquiry to interact in the process, rather than leading them to remain spectators. Pearce (2007) described spectator knowledge as attempting to understand or represent things that are "out there". Avoiding attaining knowledge as a spectator, CMM research-

23

ers focus on participatory knowledge by engaging in the process and acting as an "agent in the process of making social worlds" (p. 52).

This kind of research typically involves four steps. First, researchers listen to the community members and organize the information learned. Second, researchers, sometimes with representative community members, interpret this data and identify themes, categories, and meanings. Third, these findings are reflected back to the community to see if the interpretations make sense to the community and to refine them as well. In the fourth stage, the researchers facilitate various forms of dialogue about next steps and actions to be taken. Notice that this is a special application of DICA.

RESEARCH EXAMPLE

In 1995, the Public Dialogue Consortium entered an agreement with the City of Cupertino to begin a series of dialogues on issues of concern. In his book *Public Dialogue and Participatory Democracy: The Cupertino Community Project,* Spano (2001) summarized this project in identifying community issues and establishing community-wide dialogues over a period of years.

This community-based action research project is complex, but began with a series of four phases:

- Phase I was devoted to a series of focus groups in which citizens voiced their concerns and explored their issues. These issues were interpreted and framed at this stage.

- Phase II involved feeding this information back to community discussion groups and eliciting various ideas for visions and action plans.

- Phase III focused on providing community input to city leaders.

- Phase IV was the establishment of ongoing community dialogues on identified issues and new concerns.

---

3 | RESEARCH QUESTIONS

Maintaining a Communication Perspective

CMM research questions always take a communication perspective by focusing on interaction and looking at what is created in the process. Notice the difference in these examples:

Transmission perspective: *To what extent does an anti-drug campaign change adolescent drug-use behavior?*

Communication perspective: *How do adolescent peer groups talk about anti-drug campaign messages?*

Transmission perspective: *What strategies do people use to gain the compliance of others?*

Communication Perspective: *What forms does interaction in compliance-gaining situations take?*

Transmission perspective: *How do women and men's messages differ in marital conflict situations?*

Communication Perspective: *How do husbands and wives understand their interaction patterns in selected cases of marital conflict?*

General Guidelines for Generating Research Questions*

Here is a useful general sequence for writing good research questions:

Name your topic:

I am studying:

Imply your question:

Because I want to:

State the rationale for the questions and the project:

In order to understand:

Refine your question:

My research will yield information that will help me answer this question:

State the larger program or theme:

Which will lead me to better understand:

*Adapted from *The Craft of Research* by Wayne Booth, Joseph Williams, and Gregory Colomb, 2nd ed., 2003.

RESEARCH EXAMPLE

I am studying mediation . . .

Because I want to describe communication patterns common in mediation . . .

In order to interpret how mediators and disputants understand and respond to one another.

My research will yield information that will help me answer this question: How do participants in mediation manage conflict through communication?

Which will lead me to better understand how people create, reproduce, and change conflicts in communication.

Person Perspectives and Research Questions

Borrowing a concept from grammar, CMM identifies two perspectives from which communication can be viewed. The **first-person perspective** views the situation from the position of an actor in it. Here one is concerned with how to understand and respond to a situation: What is going on **here,** and how should **I (we)** act into this situation?" The **third-person perspective,** looking at the interaction from outside, captures observations about what is going on **there** and what we see when we observe from outside: What are **they** doing?

When we are an actor in an actual episode of communication, we normally take a first-person perspective. When we are an observer, we take the third-person perspective. These two perspectives are especially useful in writing research questions and making design and data collection decisions. The research can look quite different, depending on which perspective is taken.

First-Person Research Questions

First-person research questions are designed to elicit participants' perceptions and meanings about the interactions in which they are engaged. Here are some examples:

> What stories do middle school students tell about computers in their schools?

> How do mediators explain their role in identified cases of mediation?

> How do recovering addicts' life stories change over time in a recovery program?

Notice that first-person questions center on participants' own stories, or how they depict or express their understandings of their experience in particular episodes. The data used to answer such questions are going to be first-person accounts and stories, elicited in interviews or heard in the natural setting.

Third-Person Research Questions

Third-person questions rely on observation of what is happening:

How do students respond to instructor questions in classroom discussions?

What is the interactional structure of an initial office-visit episode for a new patient at the XYZ clinic?

What interactions lead to the first hand-holding in a new, potentially romantic, relationship between same-sex romantic partners?

Third-person questions are frequently addressed with observation data. However, you can elicit such data through interviews with others who have observed these sequences, including the participants themselves. You can, for example, ask people to take a third-person perspective and describe interactions in which they participated. For example, you might ask a teacher to tell you how students respond when they ask questions; you could interview nurses who have observed many initial office-visits to describe the episode; or you might interview same-sex couples and ask them to reflect back on when they first held hands.

Mixed Questions

A thorough research project or program will probably make use of both kinds of questions. Certainly, the DICA process requires both. Here is a simplified version of a DICA study:

Description: What is the interactional structure of an initial office-visit episode for a new patient at the XYZ clinic? (third-person)

Interpretation: (1) What meanings do patients have for such visits? (first-person) (2) What kinds of relationships do such episodes create? (third-person)

Critique: (1) What kinds of relationships do physicians and patients hope to create in such episodes? (first-person) (2) What kinds of relationships are actually created? (first-person & third-person)

Action: (1) How might initial office visits be improved so as to achieve the kinds of relationships that physicians and patients wish to create? (first-person)

Contexts for Research Questions: Where is the Focus?

After identifying the perspective to take as a researcher, you must consider the context that you will focus in, on, and/or within. As previously mentioned, focusing on interaction is a key element of CMM; yet, what part of interaction should be the focus?

Research can focus on acts, interacts, triplets, episodes, relationships, and larger contexts. Let's revisit the example discussed earlier when describing acts, interacts, and triplets. If you really want to look at the act of a student turning in homework that demonstrates the student had not read the material, what are the elements of context to consider?

29

The list is endless, but as we know from stories, we have to label something as the beginning and end since the "true" beginning and the "true" end are impossible to identify. Possible options to consider for the beginning include: the first day of the week, month, spring semester, school year, college, high school, etc. Depending on the research question, the beginning varies. Even though the story will continue through the end of the semester, school year, college life, etc., you must consider where to conclude the focus.

When focusing on **acts**, you do not simply look at an act without considering the context in which the act was performed. One example of a research question considering an act might look like the following: How do college students respond to class assignments?

For each student considered, the beginning of the context could be the distribution of the assignment criteria. The end of the context could be the submission of the assignment. The act of focus is the assignment; yet, the research question will provide information for the instructor to help understand how students make sense of the assignment criteria.

Shifting the focus to the **interact**, the research question might be the following: How do instructors respond to poor student work on assignments in a collegiate classroom?

The interact of focus consists of the students' submissions and the instructors' responses. Again, larger context helps to make sense of the response. The question will provide information to help understand how the instructors make sense of poor assignment submission in the response.

When focusing on a **triplet**, the researcher might ask the following question: How do students' respond to instructor in-class feedback on poor assignment submissions? The question will provide information to understand how students make sense of instructors' responses in class to poor assignment submission.

When broadening the context to include an **episode** of communication in this example, the triplet is considered along with other acts. One possible research question follows: How do college students and instructors manage feedback through communication? In answering the question, the researcher will look at acts, interacts, and triplets to make sense of the episode. The beginning of the episode for this question may be the initial discussion of the assignment criteria, and the final act could be the feedback when the instructor delivers a response to the assignment in the classroom.

When considering this example, one might desire to understand the relationship between instructors and students to better understand how they understand and respond to one another. With this focus, one might ask the following question: How do collegiate students and instructors understand their relationship?

In all of these questions, the object is not to provide a generalization about every college student and every college professor. Yet, each question is focused on a specific context. The outcome(s) of the research is a better understanding of the interactions at a specific institution with a specific instructor and a specific class.

Questions That Make Connections: Reflexivity

Reflexive research questions look at ways in which two or more contexts of meaning and action entail one another. For example:

How do students depict an online lecture in a structured writing response?

How do online lecturers make sense of and respond to students' structured writing responses?

31

The beauty of reflexive questions is that they lead one to investigate the ways in which context are mutually entailing, or ways in which contexts affect one another in a circular fashion. The value here is that reflexivity helps researchers avoid simplistic, linear, and causal thinking.

4 | TOOLS FOR DESCRIPTION

Describing Interactions

The Serpentine Model

The serpentine model, used primarily as a conversation or episode analysis tool, is particularly useful in depicting interactions turn-by-turn. This model arrays the moves in a conversation along a timeline shaped like a snake, hence serpentine.

This model can be used to describe an interactional sequence based on your data. Acts within an episode are laid out in a line, as A1, A2, A3, etc.:

[A1: Hi] →[A2: Hi] →[A3: How are you?] →[A4: Fine]

The first communicator's meanings (or constitutive and regulative rules) for the act are shown above the line, and the second communicator's rules appear below the line. You would normally elicit these meanings in interviews, or you might infer them from descriptions of the interaction or other documentary research.

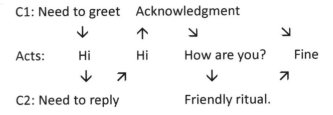

You can use the serpentine model to describe ordinary episodes or problematic ones. The model can be used to describe actual moves in a real conversation or higher level conversational moves in an ongoing set of interactions that are challenging to the participants. The "communicators" can be individual persons, groups, organizations, or even institutions, depending on the scope of the research.

This model is just meant as a heuristic device that will guide data collection and analysis. You can do this graphically, or you can accomplish the same thing in tabular or paragraph form. Whether you are doing it graphically or textually, your analysis will trace an interaction across time, indicating the meanings and rules that drive the participants to respond and act in the ways they do.

One technique for creating such an analysis is to hypothesize a serpentine based on initial information; share this with participants in an interview; and see if it resonates with them or whether they would modify the analysis is some way.

RESEARCH EXAMPLE

Pearce, Littlejohn, & Alexander (1989), along with several colleagues, conducted an extended study and critique of the political interaction between the New Religious Right (NCR) and its critics, so-called Secular Humanists, in the 1980s.

As a first stage, the researchers used a serpentine model to depict an abstracted version of this interaction across an extended episode in which the NCR interpreted the liberal agenda as institutionalized immorality and on this basis decided to "go political." The liberal critics interpreted these conservative political actions as intolerant and anti-democratic. Therewith, the liberals lectured and chastised the conservative Christians, which only made the NCR more active. This pattern continued until both sides saw that it lead nowhere, and certain attempts were then made to change the nature of the interaction. The researchers came to call this pattern "moral conflict."

Daisy Model

The serpentine analysis is used to describe an interaction, but it is normally limited to a single interaction or episode. It does not tell you much about the many conversations or relationships in which certain meanings are created. For the latter, the daisy model is especially useful.

You can take any object of interest and depict it at the center of the flower, as shown in Figure 2. Each conversation or relationship that has contributed to one's meaning for the object in the center is depicted as a petal. The atomic model is another way to illustrate the same basic idea. Typically, the atomic model identifies larger communities of which relevant to the communicator's actions, and the daisy is used to identify specific relationships or conversations.

The daisy model can also serve as a visual way of considering the conversations comprising the research data and how these conversations affect the researcher's decisions. Again, the graphic is just a heuristic to shape interpretive thinking. You can do just as well describing the conversations that impact a person's sense of self, relationship, or any other object of interest.

The daisy is also a good way to collect data. You can present the daisy to participants and have them fill in the petals; then you can "translate" their daisies into a discursive description.

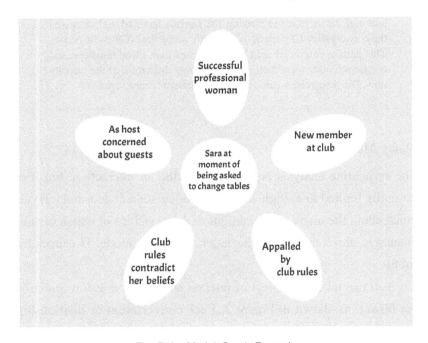

The Daisy Model: Sara's Example
Figure 2, Wasserman & Fisher-Yoshida, 2017, p. 9

36

RESEARCH EXAMPLE

In 2001, the General Assembly of the Presbyterian Church USA established a task force to study processes by which members could work through difficult issues in the church. This group created a way in which church members could dialogue about issues that might otherwise divide them. Jeff Hutcheson (2009, 2012) interviewed members of the task force and analyzed their report. He wanted to find out what social world was made in this task force process.

As he interviewed participants, Hutcheson created daisies for the various stories that they told him. Each story connected to various other people and groups. Then he looked across the daisies to note the ways in which they connected to one another. He found that many petals were the same or similar from person to person. This technique of comparing daisies enabled Hutcheson to create a sense of the social world that was constructed in the task force communication.

Collecting Descriptive Data: The Usual Suspects

Where do the data used in the serpentine and daisy models come from? The usual qualitative data methods are used—observation, interview, and textual analysis. Although it is possible to use quantitative measurement in CMM research, CMM is normally more amenable to qualitative analysis.

Observation

Especially in the description stage of research, you can gain insight by watching interactions happen or by observing recordings of interaction. The mediation research example above illustrates this technique. In this study,

The researchers were able to describe the episodic structure of mediation sessions by observing live sessions and reviewing videos of each session. A number of mediation sessions were observed and videotaped through a one-way mirror with the full knowledge and permission of the mediators and participants. The researchers carefully reviewed and analyzed the interactions that occurred in these sessions. Later, in critique and action stages, they identified potential limitations of these episodes, met with the sponsors, and explored possible improvements.

Interviews

Interviews are frequently used in CMM research. You can ask participants to describe their interactions from a third-person perspective or to explain their meanings and actions from a first-person perspective. Individual depth interviews and group interviews can be used.

RESEARCH EXAMPLE

Barnett (2011) used both observation and interviews in her research on civic engagement among college students at a European university. Barnett first observed practices at the university and in the city. She then utilized individual depth interviews to understand how students and faculty create the meaning of civic engagement. Some examples of questions included:

- How do you define civic engagement?

- How do you describe your role in civic engagement?

- Please describe one act of civic engagement in which you are involved.

Other questions provided insights unique to individual interviews. From the responses to the interviews, Barnett utilized the daisy model to make sense of the meaning of civic engagement that had been constructed in the conversations. Next, she discussed the understanding with a few students to check for understanding and write up explicit statements of their understandings of civic engagement processes. The students then decided to create a civic engagement group on campus to expand their understanding of civic engagement by implementing practices that grew out of their discussion of civic engagement.

Textual Analysis

CMM research frequently uses texts as primary data. This would be the case when the interaction itself is through texts, such as media accounts, or when there are textual depictions of situations of interest.

The study of the New Christian Right, summarized in a research example above (Pearce & Littlejohn, 1997) relied almost entirely on textual analysis. Although some interviews were conducted, the primary data consisted of third-person researcher observations of the discourse produced in this conflict and textual accounts of the conflict and participants' stories of the episodes of conflict they experienced.

5 | TOOLS FOR INTERPRETATION

Stories as Interpretive Data

The CMM storytelling model, commonly called LUUUUTT (pronounced like "loot"), is very useful in exploring social worlds. The letters in this acronym stand for (1) LIVED stories, (2) UNTOLD stories, (3) UNHEARD stories, (4) UNKNOWN stories, (5) UNTELLABLE stories, (6) TOLD stories, and (7) stories TELLING. If you find all of the U's and T's confusing, you might refer to this model as LU4T2 (Forsythe, 2012), or even more simply, "the storytelling model."

Actually, stories can be descriptive. One might begin by describing the stories told. However, more often story analysis will go beyond mere description, and the storytelling model is good for helping you understand the story dynamics of the social reality in which participants find themselves.

This model is a handy way to structure interviews or to analyze interviews and other forms of data in terms of their story value. Using the model, you can begin to address questions such as:

- How do the participants experience what is going on? (lived stories)

- From their experience, what do they tell, what can they tell, and what remains untellable?

- What stories are not told, and why?

- What told stories are not heard, and why?

- What is the group's storytelling process? When and where are stories told? How are they told?

RESEARCH EXAMPLE

In a series of fascinating simulation research studies, Lydia Forsythe (2009) formed operating-room teams to simulate surgical situations. The teams would stop from time to time to reflect on what was happening and how it might be changed. These reflections were recorded and analyzed using the storytelling model.

Through this process, teams learned how to work more collaboratively and effectively in surgical settings.

Contexts of Meaning and Action

The meaning hierarchy model depicts contexts of meaning and action in a stack design. An act is understood within a context that is itself understood within a series of higher-order contexts. For example, one's relationship with a family member might be understood within the context of caring for relatives, which, in turn, is understood within the context of family.

Researchers normally interpret the hierarchy of meanings by eliciting stories from participants. Because there is rarely only one story being told, the participant(s) are invited to share multiple stories that provide contexts for each other.

As the researcher, you will recognize that each story is informing the subsequent stories, allowing for a rich analysis of meaning-making. You may ask questions like "So how does your understanding of the family influence your feelings about taking care of relatives?" or "How would you define your relationship with those you take care of?" For such an analysis, you would allow these hierarchies to be multiple and potentially conflicting at several points during an episode.

RESEARCH EXAMPLE

Laura Burton (2016) looked at the ways in which hope is constructed in a community based support program, which offers wide ranging self-help programs in such areas as addiction, anger management, grief, divorce, chronic illness, relational problems, and stress and anxiety. The program consists of 6 to 13 weekly 2-hour large- and small-group sessions. Using CMM as a basis, Burton addressed the communication processes that facilitate hope, the stories that participants tell as part of the development of hope, and the communication patterns that emerged in the sessions.

Using an appreciative approach, the researcher observed and recorded sessions and interviewed participants and facilitators. Burton conducted a thematic analysis, in which she interpreted the themes that emerged in interviews into meaning clusters, particularly focusing on the stories told. She transcribed the recorded sessions and completed an episode analysis, in which she identified narratives as meaning-making strategies, using the hierarchy of meaning model of CMM.

With redemption stories predominant in the construction of hope, Burton's participants identified three important communication processes—(1) reflexive moments, in which individuals achieved an epiphany about the possibility of moving from despair to hope; (2) transitional messages, or bifurcation points in one's narrative; and (3) story space, in which stories come together to create something new. These processes seem to involve a deep, redemptive sharing of stories.

Borrowing from ornithology, Burton likened the group process to murmurations, in which a flock of starlings coordinate their flight in ways that create amazing patterns in the sky. This action is entirely social, although researchers do not yet know exactly how the birds coordinate their actions in this way. You cannot predict exactly what patterns will be created, but the "creative" potential of the flock in flight is undeniable. With this new metaphor, Burton adds a new way of understanding the coordinated management of meaning.

Logical Force

Described as "oughtness", logical force informs choices based on the compulsion to act or not to act in certain ways. The analysis of logical force falls along the four types:

- Prefigurative Force

Based on the prior actions/words/meanings of others, I/we must do <X>. Sometimes called "causal force," this logic is experienced as having one's actions caused by previous ones. Example: My brother always bullied me, so I am shy in social situations.

- Contextual Force

Based on the situation I/we are in, I/we must do <X>. Here the force is from the context to the act. In this situation, we are compelled to act as we do. Example: We are fighters in our family; that's just the way we are.

- Practical Force

Based on the desired outcome, I/we must do <X>. This is practical thinking: Do X to accomplish Y. Example: I want my kids to get into a great preparatory school, so I hired a tutor for them.

- Implicative / Reflexive Force

I/we want to affect the context of my/our actions, so I/we must do <X>. Here the idea is to change the context itself in some way. Example: I was so shy in high school, but I want to be confident as a person in college, so I am going to be more outgoing.

Loops

Borrowing from particle physics, Pearce and Cronen identified two common types of loops—charmed and strange. A charmed loop is self-reinforcing. One's actions reify on one's meanings, and one's meanings reproduce one's actions. In a strange loop, meanings and actions disconfirm one another.

An alcoholic may come to create a story that enables sobriety by connecting non-drinking with the belief that he or she is powerless against drinking. This is a charmed loop: Alcohol is bad for me, I am powerless against it, and therefore I do not drink.

However, many alcoholics are engaged in a strange loop, in which their meanings and actions keep changing, leading to a repetitive pattern of drinking and not drinking. Strange loops can be depicted by diagrams of conversation that oscillate between shifting contexts of meaning and action, see Figure 1.

This produces a flow of conversation that is repetitive, circular, and confusing. Researchers can use strange loops in a visual way to illustrate hierarchies of meaning that are not completely singular at each level, and articulate particular contexts and place value upon them.

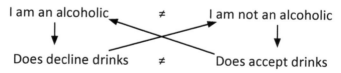

The Strange Loop: An Alcoholic's Dilemma
Figure 1, Pearce, Sostrin, & Pearce, 2011, p. 24

The Reflecting team

As a research tool for interpretation, the reflecting team provides multiple perspectives (conversations) to examine data and provide insight. In general, the research team examines data and also provides process knowledge to improve subsequent data collection. The researcher(s)' social worlds are enriched by conversations with and among members of the group. Reflecting teams' interactions are usually free-form. Members are encouraged to play with the data and be creative and spontaneous in suggesting various interpretations.

As you will note, the process and details are vague; many are up to the researcher(s) in question. Ultimately, it is a process that involves multiple perspectives and allows for any number of configurations on the way to enriching understandings of the social worlds created in the research setting.

RESEARCH EXAMPLE

In the aftermath of a hot civil conflict in Maluku, Indonesia, a group of non-profit agencies convened a five-day Interfaith Peacebuilding Institute, in which parties to the conflict came together to have dialogue on rebuilding their communities. As part of an action-research project, Lowry and Littlejohn (2006) studied the social worlds created in the process and the process in which these were co-constructed.

The researchers used several forms of data, including direct observation and field notes taken by research assistants. Reflecting teams were used in two ways. Each day after the session ended, the facilitators and research assistants convened privately to reflect on what had happened and to process their observations. Participant reflecting teams were also built into the process. At the conclusion of each day's activities, a different set of participants converged into a circle, while other participants listened to their reflections. The facilitator asked the group questions that enabled them to reflect on and share their understandings of what had happened that day.

Careful notes were taken on each of these types of reflection groups and later used as a kind of data to include in the final analysis.

6 | TOOLS FOR CRITIQUE AND ACTION

Bifurcation Points

Bifurcation points occur when critical choices are made. Other terms for bifurcation points are *critical moments* and *choice points*. When such moments are important, the choice of how to respond will have a significant impact on whatever may occur next. Such moments are important in determining the social world made.

When utilizing bifurcation points, a researcher can have individuals consider difficult decisions in an episode (i.e. relationships). By visually displaying or talking through such critical choices, people are able to (re)consider their choice and options at that point. When working with a group, visually representing or discussing each person's critical choices helps each member and other members to better understand his/her and others' decisions and actions. Through the exercise of identifying points, the researcher helps members manage meaning and recreate their story. Below is a simplified example of an individual process.

Individual Process: When I arrived to donate blood, the woman was rude and did not explain the process to me, so I left.

Choice Point: Stay and donate, leave, or do something else.

Choices to consider for future decisions at critical points: Go through with the process of donating blood without information; leave without enough information and do not donate blood; ask for information about the process of donating blood and choose to donate or not; ask for a moment to consider the process before deciding; ask others who are donating blood about previous experiences and the process; etc.

Evaluating Worlds Made

Researchers can also help individuals to evaluate existing social worlds. As a researcher, one can ask individuals to describe the existing components of the situation (i.e. classroom environment). Providing a list of current resources, practices, and forces allows the members to see the context of the existing social world. Then, researchers can ask members to evaluate the existing position of the social world. By evaluating, individuals will see that others agree that change is needed or not needed in the existing social world. Below is an example of evaluating the current social world of a lecture style classroom.

Classroom Example: What educational world is being made by the communication patterns in this classroom?

Patterns: Have to be in class on time or before; have to sit and listen to a long, boring lecture; have to regurgitate the information on quizzes and tests; do not get to relate concepts to my life; do not get to add information from my experiences; do not get to interact during lecture; do not get any excused absences; etc.

Forces imposing the actions: Hierarchical status of lecturer; hierarchical status of the academic system; the rules and regulations identified on the syllabus including the attendance policy that allows no flexibility with tardies or absences.

World being made: Education is transmission of information in a highly disciplined and structured environment. Communication is primarily one-way and outcome oriented.

RESEARCH EXAMPLE

In his dissertation, Noblet (2015) studied the communication process in email to provide some understanding of the creation of digital social worlds at organizations. There were three main outcomes that guided his study. First, the work created an exemplar study that utilized a general CMM framework in the DICA form for analysis, in the hopes that others will utilize CMM as a research method. Second, the study provided organizations a template for the study of email. Thirdly, this dissertation provided a process-based understanding of digital social world creation.

To achieve these outcomes, this research used CMM as a theory and a method. Noblet employed a reflexive researcher orientation through the duration of study and understood organizational culture as shared meaning co- constructed by conversational participants over time. He used the DICA method to coordinate the research efforts.

Noblet identified communication patterns in Enron executive email conversations and the patterns' contributions to the Enron executive cultures. Through the process he identified bifurcation points and choices made at those points. He then explored how different choices at the identified bifurcation points could have contributed to more positive cultures.

Visioning Preferred Alternative Patterns

Researchers may find unwanted repetitive patterns in episodes explored in their studies. At this point—in the critique stage—participants could engage in dialogue to explore better social worlds and more effective patterns of interaction. By creating a list, the individual(s) has desirable aspects that could replace undesirable elements of the existing social world to create a better social world. Researchers demonstrate an active role in the research by assisting in the process of creating alternative patterns. By visioning alternative patterns, people are able to see other ways of interacting. Then, individuals can see which alternative pattern is preferred and discuss ways of shifting unwanted patterns to the preferred alternative pattern. Here is an example that continues from the example above:

> Alternative patterns that could lead to desirable resources and practices: being in class on time or before; sitting, listening, and interacting with the material presented; demonstrating knowledge attained through personal examples and course concepts on quizzes and tests; participating in class with the material to add information and examples of course material; sharing information in small groups occasionally, etc.

> Forces at play: Sense of individuality and value in students' experience, education through interactivity, etc.

> World created: A comfortable and safe learning environment in which all participants feel that they contributed to a positive learning experience.

Acting Intentionally

After considering a preferred alternative pattern, an essential component to assisting individuals as a researcher is helping to create an action plan. Researchers want individuals to answer the question, how do we take what we found in research and put it into practice? Visual brainstorming is effective here. One might start with the end ideal and work backwards to determine what the individuals can intentionally do to attain the preferred patterns.

RESEARCH EXAMPLE

In her dissertation, Archiopoli (2014) studied patterns that lead to stigma in healthcare situations, including but not limited to feeling bullied, excluded, rejected, blamed, or embarrassed due to a health condition the participants or someone they knew possessed. In interviews, she elicited stories of stigma-producing episodes and what the interactions within such episodes meant to the participants. The study was organized around the DICA model, in which participants described episodes of stigma, interpreted meanings and actions within these episodes, critiqued these patterns, and explored options for improvement.

In later interviews and/or focus groups, participants spent some time looking at how different patterns might be created in healthcare settings. She utilized grounded theory to analyze the interview data; themes and subthemes emerged to reveal the patterned nature of health-related stigma

Archiopoli concluded that the major findings of her study were the patterned nature of health-related stigma, and further that these patterns could be interrupted and reconstructed in a way that reframes negative experiences and promotes a more positive perspective for approaching issues of health-related stigma.

7 | SEAVA IN RESEARCH

Overview

We provided a brief overview of the SEAVA process earlier in this manual. Here we look more closely at SEAVA as a powerful research tool. SEAVA can be thought of as a stepwise, yet iterative, process in which each step builds and informs the next stage and previous ones. Recall that SEAVA stands for (1) storyboarding, (2) enriching, (3) analyzing, (4) visioning, and (5) acting. It is really just a more detailed and refined form of DICA.

Storyboarding

In general, storyboarding is preceded by awareness building, in which the researcher invites the research subject to embrace an attitude of curiosity and to pay attention to experiences in a way that might not have occurred before. The general goal of the S in SEAVA is to define the episode(s) of communication in question and describe what happened in a turn-by-turn manner. In consulting, this is done graphically with a documentation process (including post-it notes or other materials), such that the details are distanced from the participant(s) and the focus is on process. The three sub-components of this approach are as follows: specifically identifying the key episode(s), documenting the episode(s), and punctuating the episode(s). In research, there is a bit more creative freedom in each step, but the overall goals remain the same.

Identifying the episode(s)

In this phase, you as the researcher are asking questions to get at the pattern of communication that has given rise to the meanings under investigation. This is an assumption of this methodology; that is, there is a communicative pattern that is producing the phenomenon under investigation. The overriding question, asked in many different ways, will then be "How did this get made?" In general, avoiding close-ended and summative questions earlier in the questioning is best, and allows the conversation to explore many different avenues in route to meaning construction. These explorations can focus on the specifics of episode(s), including the who/what/where/when, and the separation of people from the phenomena.

Documenting the key episode(s)

As a researcher, you will more than likely be recording the interactions under investigation in some manner. SEAVA, specifically storyboarding, asks that you pay attention to this recording process, and do so in a graphic manner that invites participation by those you are interacting with. While the form is not as important, the concepts are important. You should demonstrate the turn-by-turn progression in an episode or series of episodes and invite collaborative editing and revision until an agreed-upon sequence is established. This can use a physical storyboard and post-it notes, or a whiteboard and dry erase markers, or any number of materials. Your episodes will probably receive many additions and subtractions throughout the process, but make sure these are visible as each phase of SEAVA is practiced.

Punctuating the episode(s)

Finally, punctuation of the episode(s) involves agreement about the start and end of a particular phenomenon. Since you have made the turns and episode(s) visible, as noted above, the question you may ask is "are all the elements of each story visible, and if not, what have we left off?" The goal is to ensure that the details of the episode(s) are captured, and the beginning/ending of the sequence is agreed upon by the research participant(s).

Enriching

At this phase of SEAVA, there are two research tools that are available to assist the researcher – the LUUUUTT and the daisy model. Each does something different, but ultimately enriches the details previously identified in storyboarding. First, work with the LUUUUTT model, and then proceed to the daisy model. Remember, as a researcher you have the design choice to embrace all or none of these steps; this is presented purely as a progression in accordance with the consulting manual. Also, during this process your research may go back to storyboarding; that is not unexpected, nor uncommon.

LUUUUTT – Story naming and pattern revealing

While described in detail earlier in this manual, LUUUUTT's purpose at this stage is to identify other stories which are informing the episode(s) under investigation. The purposes of LUUUUTT also include highlighting the tension between the lived and told episode(s) and the manner of storytelling.

Daisy – Describing the social system

As a researcher, the daisy model invites exploration of a social system, but your choice will be which social system is most beneficial to investigate. Perhaps you want to investigate a particular sub-culture, or workgroup, or interpersonal affiliation; whatever your choice, be sure to invite participation by the participant(s) to help identify who, and also to identify what elements of the daisy model are visible to which people.

Analyzing

In the analyzing phase of SEAVA, there are three main steps for the researcher to follow: (1) display the hierarchy of stories, (2) examine the logical force that holds the episode(s) together, and (3) explore the episode(s)' features. Each step is itself an analysis section, and can be included in the research report as such. You are taking the data you have gathered in storyboarding and enriching, and making CMM arguments about the stories present.

Displaying the hierarchy of stories

The goal of this analysis is to demonstrate that multiple stories are unequal, even if they are related – some stories function as context for other stories. As a researcher, you will not only want to explicate this hierarchy and interrelatedness of stories, but also to invite research participants to arrange them and speak to the stories at different hierarchical levels. For example, you will identify each story in detail and describe its relationships to other stories, and then have the participants arrange pieces of paper with the stories on them and arrange them in order of importance. This will change the conversation and allow for deeper analysis of the stories and their relationships to one another.

Examining logical force

As you are aware, logical force can be considered oughtness – it is the force behind choices, the compelling feeling of empowerment or prohibition. The use of questioning comes in centrally, and as a researcher you might ask about similar situations that invoked feelings of oughtness, or hypothetical situations. Either way, you are attempting to get at the participant(s)' understanding of how the logical forces influenced the meaning-making process.

Exploring episodic features

Once all of the above steps have been completed (not necessarily the only time or entirely), an exploration of the combination of descriptive features is appropriate. This is called the serpentine model, and is discussed in the 2007 *Making Social Worlds* (Pearce) text. Simply stated, the serpentine model is a combination of the storyboard step, with the addition of logical force and hierarchy of meaning. At this point, the researcher is able to construct a social world containing the participants, and make arguments about the forms, elements, and facets of that social world. From this point, you begin to make judgments about the process, and potentially, how to improve and make better social worlds, which are the next two steps.

Visioning

In the consulting process, visioning is the open brainstorming process that invites participants to imagine a preferred situation of interaction and meaning, in essence, to imagine a preferred social world. For researchers, this process can be thought of as the "discussion" section of a research article; it is the recommendations based on the analysis provided earlier in the SEAVA process. You can choose to involve the research participant(s) at this juncture or not; the tools outlined below can be used individually or in collaboration.

The desired situation

What changes would have the greatest effect in creating a desired situation? What elements or details need to be included to realize such a desired situation? These can be non-tangible and include concepts like trust, harmony or justice; they can also be tangible, including things like space requirements, interaction rules, or others.

Appreciation

What facets of the current situation are most beneficial or important to the situation? What would occur if these were norms or dominant stories within an episode? These questions can be answered in appreciation of the present research context.

Alteration

What differences would be present if something were to change? Which things specifically could change for the better? What bifurcation points (critical moments of choice) exist and how do their outcomes affect the situation? All these questions guide the alteration process.

Symbolic construction

What images and/or metaphors would be appropriate in the research context? What images/metaphors could change the situation or meaning? This section invites the researcher to use symbols as a way of telling deeper and more sophisticated stories for better social worlds.

Acting

Finally, the acting phase concludes the SEAVA process. If visioning is the discussion section of a research article, acting is the future research and/or directions section. In consulting, acting is the conclusion and summation of the transformative process, resulting in shift of the meaning being made. For researchers, acting can be considered writing changes into the conversation. As a result of the research conducted, the academic conversation may have changed, and might now include parts and concepts established by the research. This section can include comments about moving forward, and what could/ should/might happen in future academic endeavors.

RESEARCH EXAMPLE

In her dissertation, Barnett (2014) employed the SEAVA model when working with a health care team to enhance the process of Diagnosis Delivery of Autism Spectrum Disorders (ASD). Her general goal was to investigate how professionals at an early childhood diagnostic center in the southwest could co-construct an effective and efficient process of delivering diagnosis of ASD to parent(s), caregiver(s), and/or family member(s). Another goal was to modify and utilize the existing theory of CMM for an academic research setting and provide another possible methodological approach for other research studies.

To attain her goals, Barnett utilized CMM as a theory and method. The theoretical framework provided the communication perspective and understanding that the researcher was a part of the process that facilitated the process of understanding. The method provided several heuristics to collect and analyze data. The SEAVA model was the main model used in the research; yet she incorporated other CMM heuristics throughout the process, which included: the daisy model, the hierarchy model, the Serpentine model, and the LUUUTT model.

Barnett's data collection methods included: observations, individual interviews, and a group interview. Episodes of observation were discussed during the individual interviews; the understanding of the episodes was enhanced through individual interviews; and the collection of understanding of the episodes of communication was discussed in the group interview. Through a reflexive process, the study explained how the diagnostic team created meaning by identifying their communication patterns, rules of symbol use, rules of meaning and action, strengths and weakness of the process, and individual and team goals.

8 | USING CMM CREATIVELY

THIS MANUAL DESCRIBES A WIDE variety of ways to use CMM creatively. Through this manual, you have seen brief examples and suggestions of research questions and contexts where CMM may be applied. Below we provide some contexts where CMM could provide a unique and useful framework.

1. Situations where individuals are confused and unclear about resources and practices (i.e. students trying to donate blood)

2. Situations that have a lot of coordination but little coherence (i.e. a lecture class environment)

3. Situations where information is coherent, but the sharing of the coherence is unknown (i.e. media campaigns)

4. Situations where change is needed (i.e. poor scores on exams)

5. Situations that have a lot of mystery (i.e. why smokers who understand the dangers of smoking and the available resources continue to smoke)

6. Situations where individuals from one culture do not communicate effectively with individuals from a different culture (i.e. patients who do not understand medical jargon used by physicians)

7. Situations where force constrains effective communication (i.e. in an interpersonal relationship where power inequality is present)

8. Situations that participate in unwanted repetitive patterns (i.e. victims in abusive relationships that continue to stay with abusive partners)

9. Situations where multiple channels are utilized for effective coherence, yet lack coherence (i.e. organizations that utilize a variety of online tools—instant messaging, email, and website messaging—to distribute company information; yet, employees are confused about messages and do not have full coherence)

10. Situations that prompt the following questions: What are we making; how are we making it in communication; and how can we make it better?

REFERENCES

Archiopoli, A. (2014). *Don't put me in "Quotes": Examining communication episodes of health-related stigma.* (Ph.D. Dissertation, Albuquerque: University of New Mexico).

Barnett, N.A. (2011). *Broadening the horizon: An ethnography utilizing CMM to establish an intercultural collaboration focused on civic engagement.* (Master's Thesis, Indiana University Purdue University Indianapolis).

Barnett, N.A. (2014). *The process of diagnosis delivery of Autism Spectrum Disorders.* (Ph.D. Dissertation, Albuquerque: University of New Mexico).

Baxter, L. A. & Babbie, E. (2004). The basics of communication research. Belmont, CA: Wadsworth/Thompson Learning.

Booth, W., Williams, J, & Colomb, G. (2003). *The craft of research.* Chicago: University of Chicago Press.

Burton, L. L. (2016). *Hope and the duality of narrative: The communication processes facilitating hope at a community-based support program.* (Ph.D. Dissertation, Albuquerque: University of New Mexico).

Cronen, V. (2001) Practical theory, practical art, and the pragmatic-systemic account of inquiry, *Communication Theory,* 11, 14-35.

Cronen, V.E. & Pearce, W.B. (1981). Logical force in interpersonal communication: A new concept of the 'necessity' in social behavior, *Communication,* 6, 5-67.

Hample, D. (2008). Issue forum: Can we enhance people's lives? *Communication Monographs, 75*(4) 319-350.

Lindlof, T. R., & Taylor, B. C. (2011). Qualitative communication research methods (3rd ed.).Thousand Oaks, CA: Sage.

Littlejohn, S. W. (2009). Coordinated management of meaning. In S. W. Littlejohn & K. A. Foss, (Ed.), Encyclopedia of Communication Theory (vol. 1, pp. 200-203). Thousand Oaks, CA: Sage.

Noblet, N. (2015). *Email and Enron: Using CMM to make better social worlds in organizations*. (Ph.D. Dissertation, Albuquerque: University of New Mexico).

Pearce, B., & Cronen, V. (1980). *Communication, Action, and Meaning*.

Pearce, B., Sostrin, J., & Pearce, K. (2011). CMM solutions: Field guide for consultants. USA: You Get What You Make Publishing.

Pearce, W. B. (1989). Communication and the human condition. Carbondale, IL: Southern Illinois University Press.

Pearce, W. B. (2007). Making social worlds: a communication perspective. Malden, MA: Blackwell Publishing.

Pearce, W.B., & Cronen, V.E. (1980). Communication, action and meaning: The creation of social realities. NY, NY: Praeger.

Pearce, W. B., & Pearce, K.A. (2000). Extending the theory of the coordinated management of meaning (CMM) through a community dialogue process. *Communication Theory*, 405-423.

Raboin, W.E. (2010). The social construction of collaborative practice in a hospital unit. (Doctoral dissertation, Fielding Graduate University).

Salmon, G., & Faris, J. (2006). Multiagency collaboration, multiple levels of meaning: social constructionism and the CMM model as tools to further our understanding. *Journal of family therapy, 28*(3), 272-292.

Sostrin, J., Pearce, W. B., & Pearce, K. (2012). CMM Solutions – Field Guide. Online: lulu.com.

Wasserman, I.C., & Fisher-Yoshida, B. (2017.) Communicating possibilities: A brief introduction to the coordinated management of meaning. Chagrin Falls, OH: Taos Institute Publications.

TAOS INSTITUTE PUBLICATIONS

See all the Taos Publications at
www.taosinstitute.net/taos-books-and-publications

Taos Institute Publications Books in Print

* * * * * * *

Taos Tempo Series:
Collaborative Practices for Changing Times

The Magic of Organizational Life, (2017) by Mette Vinther Larsen

Paths to Positive Aging: Dog Days with a Bone and Other Essays, (2017) by Mary Gergen and Kenneth J. Gergen

70Candles! Women Thriving in Their 8th Decade, (2015) by Jane Giddan and Ellen Cole (also available as an e-book)

U&ME: Communicating in Moments that Matter, New & Revised! (2014) by John Stewart (also available as an e-book)

Relational Leading: Practices for Dialogically Based Collaboration, (2013) by Lone Hersted and Kenneth J. Gergen (also available as an e-book)

Retiring But Not Shy: Feminist Psychologists Create their Post-Careers, (2012) edited by Ellen Cole and Mary Gergen (also available as an e-book)

Developing Relational Leadership: Resources for Developing Reflexive Organizational Practices, (2012) by Carsten Hornstrup, Jesper Loehr-Petersen, Joergen Gjengedal Madsen, Thomas Johansen, Allan Vinther Jensen (also available as an e-book)

Practicing Relational Ethics in Organizations, (2012) by Gitte Haslebo and Maja Loua Haslebo

Healing Conversations Now: Enhance Relationships with Elders and Dying Loved Ones, (2011) by Joan Chadbourne and Tony Silbert

Riding the Current: How to Deal with the Daily Deluge of Data, (2010) by Madelyn Blair

Ordinary Life Therapy: Experiences from a Collaborative Systemic Practice, (2009) by Carina Håkansson

Mapping Dialogue: Essential Tools for Social Change, (2008) by Marianne "Mille" Bojer, Heiko Roehl, Mariane Knuth-Hollesen, and Colleen Magner

Positive Family Dynamics: Appreciative Inquiry Questions to Bring Out the Best in Families, (2008) by Dawn Cooperrider Dole, Jen Hetzel Silbert, Ada Jo Mann, and Diana Whitney

* * * * * * *

Focus Book Series

Coordinated Management of Meaning (CMM): A Research Manual (2017) by Natasha A. Rascon and Stephen W. Littlejohn

Communicating Possibilities: Brief Introduction to the Coordinated Management of Meaning (CMM), (2017) by Ilene C. Wasserman & Beth Fisher Yoshida

A Student's Guide to Clinical Supervision: You are not Alone, (2014) by Glenn E. Boyd (also available as an e-book)

When Stories Clash: Addressing Conflict with Narrative Mediation, (2013) by Gerald Monk, and John Winslade (also available as an e-book)

Bereavement Support Groups: Breathing Life into Stories of the Dead, (2012) by Lorraine Hedtke (also available as an e-book)

The Appreciative Organization, Revised Edition (2008) by Harlene Anderson, David Cooperrider, Kenneth J. Gergen, Mary Gergen, Sheila McNamee, Jane Watkins, and Diana Whitney

Appreciative Inquiry: A Positive Approach to Building Cooperative Capacity, (2005) by Frank Barrett and Ronald Fry (also available as an e-book)

Dynamic Relationships: Unleashing the Power of Appreciative Inquiry in Daily Living, (2005) by Jacqueline Stavros and Cheri B. Torres

Appreciative Sharing of Knowledge: Leveraging Knowledge Management for Strategic Change, (2004) by Tojo Thatchenkery

Social Construction: Entering the Dialogue, (2004) by Kenneth J. Gergen, and Mary Gergen (also available as an e-book)

Appreciative Leaders: In the Eye of the Beholder, (2001) edited by Marge Schiller, Bea Mah Holland, and Deanna Riley

Experience AI: A Practitioner's Guide to Integrating Appreciative Inquiry and Experiential Learning, (2001) by Miriam Ricketts and Jim Willis

* * * * * * *

Books for Professionals Series

Social Constructionist Perspectives on Group Work, (2015) edited by Emerson F. Rasera

New Horizons in Buddhist Psychology: Relational Buddhism for Collaborative Practitioners, (2010) edited by Maurits G.T. Kwee

Positive Approaches to Peacebuilding: A Resource for Innovators, (2010) edited by Cynthia Sampson, Mohammed Abu-Nimer, Claudia Liebler, and Diana Whitney

Social Construction on the Edge: 'Withness'—Thinking & Embodiment, (2010) by John Shotter

Joined Imagination: Writing and Language in Therapy, (2009) by Peggy Penn

Celebrating the Other: A Dialogic Account of Human Nature, (reprint 2008) by Edward Sampson

Conversational Realities Revisited: Life, Language, Body and World, (2008) by John Shotter

Horizons in Buddhist Psychology: Practice, Research and Theory, (2006) edited by Maurits Kwee, Kenneth J. Gergen, and Fusako Koshikawa

Therapeutic Realities: Collaboration, Oppression and Relational Flow, (2005) by Kenneth J. Gergen

SocioDynamic Counselling: A Practical Guide to Meaning Making, (2004) by R. Vance Peavy

Experiential Exercises in Social Construction – A Fieldbook for Creating Change, (2004) by Robert Cottor, Alan Asher, Judith Levin, and Cindy Weiser

Dialogues About a New Psychology, (2004) by Jan Smedslund

* * * * * * *

67

Spirituality, Social Construction and Relational Processes: Essays and Reflections (PDF version 2016) edited by Duane Bidwell.

Therapy as a Hermeneutic and Constructionist Dialogue: Practices of freedom and of deco-construction in the relational, language and meaning games (PDF version 2016) by Gilberto Limon (Translated from Spanish)

Recovered Without Treatment: The Process of Abandoning Crystal Meth Use Without Professional Help (PDF version 2016) by Pavel Nepustil

Introduction to Group Dynamics: Social Construction Approach to Organizational Development and Community Revitalization, (PDF version 2016), by Toshio Sugiman

Recursos psico-sociales para el post-conflicto" (Psico-social resources for post-conflict) (PDF version 2016), Edited by Angela Maria Estrada

Buddha As Therapist: Meditations (PDF version 2015), by G.T. Maurits Kwee

Diálogos para la transformación: experiencias en terapia y Otras intervenciones psicosociales en Iberoamérica – Volumen 1 and 2 (PDF version 2015), by Dora Fried Schnitman, Editora

Education as Social Construction: Contributions to Theory, Research and Practice (PDF version 2015) Editors: Thalia Dragonas, Kenneth J. Gergen, Sheila McNamee, Eleftheria Tseliou

Psychosocial Innovation in Post-War Sri Lanka (PDF version 2015) by Laurie Charles and Gameela Samarasinghe

Social Accountability & Selfhood (PDF version 2015, original publication date – 1984, Basil Blackwell, Inc.) by John Shotter

Construccionismo Social Y Discusion De Paradrigmas En Psycologia: Indeterminacion, Holismo y Juegos de Lenguaje vs. La Teoria Pictorica del Lenguaje (PDF versión 2015) by Roberto Aristequi

{In}Credible Leadership: A Guide for Shared Understanding and Application (PDF version 2015) by Yuzanne Mare, Isabel Meyer, Elonya Niehaus-Coetzee, Johann Roux

Etnia Terapéutica: Integrando Entornos (PDF version 2015) by Jeannette Samper A. and José Antonio Garciandía I.

Post-modern Education & Development (Chinese edition, PDF version 2014) Introduction by Shi-Jiuan Wu (後現代教育與發展　　介紹 吳熙琄)

Exceeding Expectations: An Anthology of Appreciative Inquiry Stories in Education from Around the World (PDF version 2014) Story Curators: Dawn Dole, Matthew Moehle, and Lindsey Godwin

The Discursive Turn in Social Psychology (PDF version 2014), by Nikos Bozatzis & Thalia Dragonas (Eds.)

Happily Different: Sustainable Educational Change – A Relational Approach (PDF version 2014), by Loek Schoenmakers

Strategising through Organising: The Significance of Relational Sensemaking, (PDF version 2013), by Mette Vinther Larsen

Therapists in Continuous Education: A Collaborative Approach, (PDF version 2013), by Ottar Ness

Contextualizing Care: Relational Engagement with/in Human Service Practices, (PDF version 2013), by Janet Newbury

Nuevos Paradigmas, Cultura y Subjetividad, by Dora Fried Schnitman

Novos Paradigmas Em Mediação (PDF versión 2013, original publicación date 1999), Dora Fried Schnitman y Stephen LittleJohn (editors)

Filo y Sofía En Diálogo: La poesía social de la conversación terapéutica (PDF version 2013, original publicación date 2000), Klaus G. Deissler y Sheila McNamee (editors). Traducción al español: Mario O. Castillo Rangel

Socially Constructing God: Evangelical Discourse on Gender and the Divine (PDF version 2013), by Landon P. Schnabel

Ohana and the Creation of a Therapeutic Community (PDF version 2013), by Celia Studart Quintas

From Nonsense Syllables to Holding Hands: Sixty Years as a Psychologist (PDF version 2013), by Jan Smedslund

Management and Organization: Relational Alternatives to Individualism (PDF version 2013, reprinted with permission) Edited by Dian Marie Hosking, H. Peter Dachler, Kenneth J. Gergen

Appreciative Inquiry to Promote Local Innovations among Farmers Adapting to Climate Change (PDF version 2013) by Shayamal Saha

La terapia Multi–Being. Una prospettiva relazionale in psicoterapia, (PDF version 2013) by Diego Romaioli

Psychotherapy by Karma Transformation: Relational Buddhism and Rational Practice (PDF version 2013) by G.T. Maurits Kwee

La terapia como diálogo hermenéutico y construccionista: Márgenes de libertad y deco-construcción en los juegos relacionales, de lenguaje y de significado (PDF versión 2012) by Gilberto Limón Arce

Wittgenstein in Practice: His Philosophy of Beginnings, and Beginnings, and Beginnings (PDF version 2012) by John Shotter

Social Construction of the Person (PDF version 2012). Editors: Kenneth J. Gergen and Keith M. Davis, Original copyright date: 1985, Springer-Verlag, New York, Inc.

Images of Man (PDF version 2012, original copyright date: 1975) by John Shotter. Methuen, London.

Ethical Ways of Being (PDF version 2012). By Dirk Kotze, Johan Myburg, Johann Roux, and Associates. Original copyright date: 2002, Ethics Alive, Institute for Telling Development, Pretoria, South Africa.

Piemp (PDF version 2012), by Theresa Hulme. Published in Afrikaans.

For book information and ordering, visit Taos Institute Publications at:
www.taosinstitutepublications.net

For further information, call: 1-888-999-TAOS, 1-440-338-6733
Email: info@taosinstitute.net